Jonathan's alpha-numeric doodles

By Jonathan Jay Brandstater

For Lisa

Introduction

This book is interactive. You may use it as a coloring book and even add your own doodles and drawings to the pages. You can also use the various letters and numbers as inspiration for your own designs.

I have used a variety of techniques while creating Jonathan's alpha-numeric doodle book: negative space, drawing in 3D, a method called ZenTangle ™ and just plain doodling. With negative space, I use shadow and contrast to define an object, rather than drawing the object itself. Drawing in 3D does not mean literally drawing in three dimensions but creating designs in such a way as to give the illusion of depth or height. Objects drawn in this way seem to pop off the page. ZenTangle ™ is a method for creating designs using simple, repetitive patterns. This technique has a way of putting one in a relaxed, meditative frame of mind. It is also therapeutic. Doodling itself is therapeutic in its own right, as well as being a lot of fun.

Enjoy!

Best wishes, Jonathan J. Brandstater
Summer, 2015

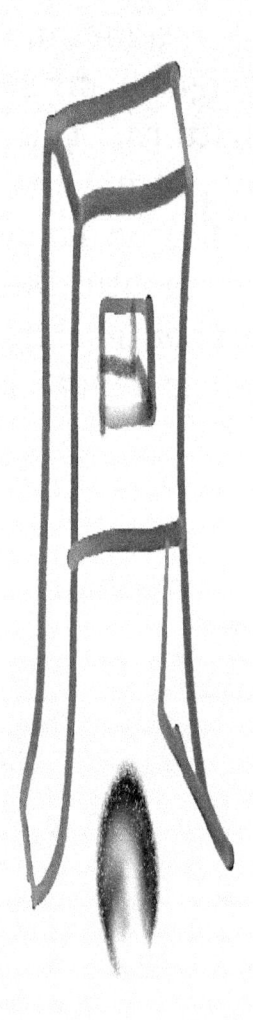

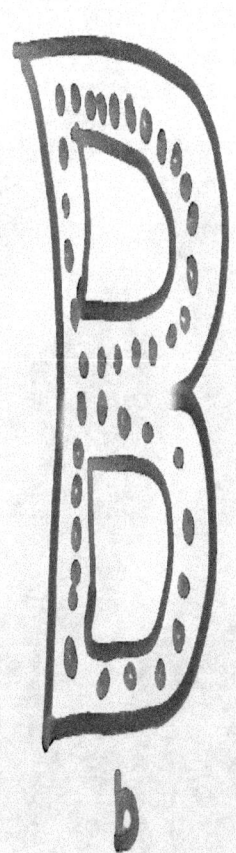

b

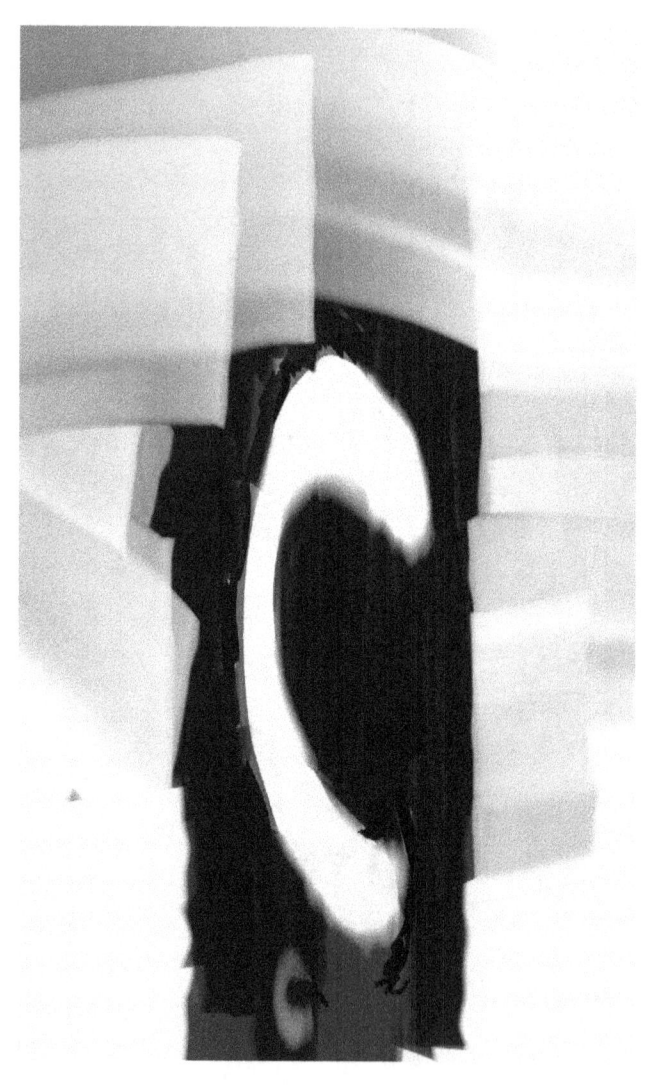

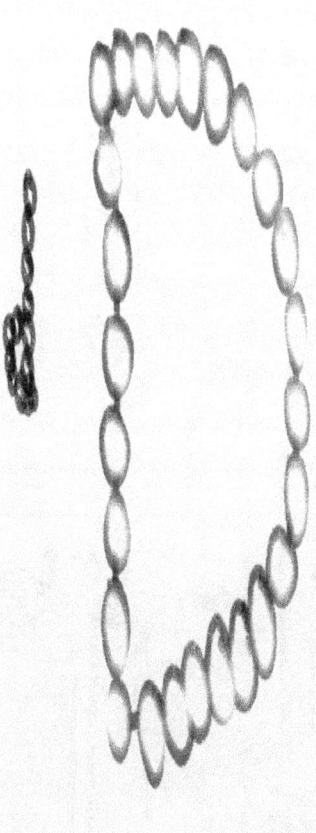

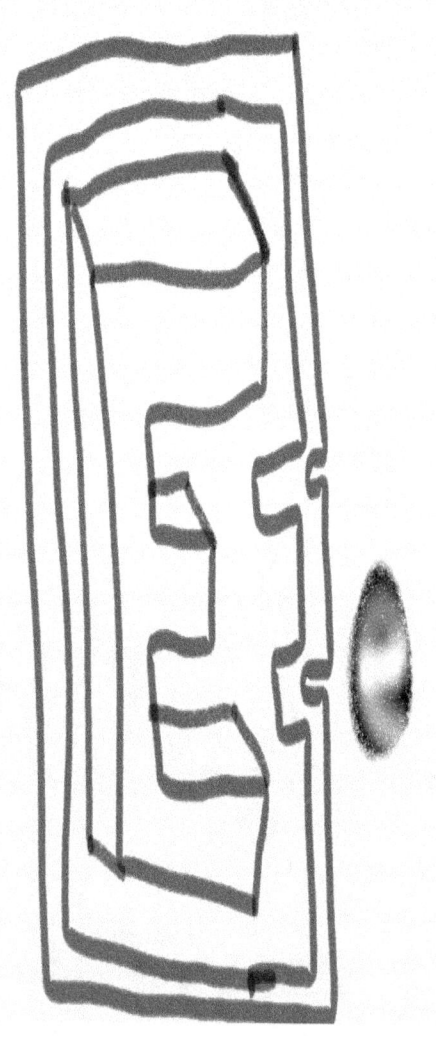

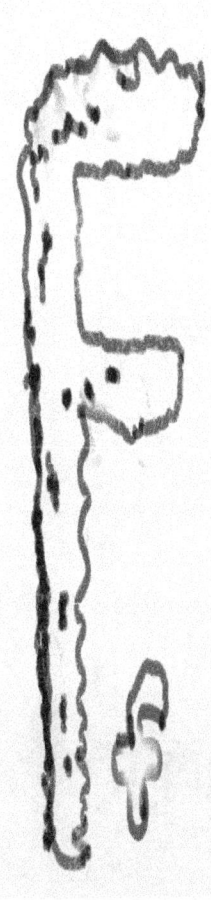

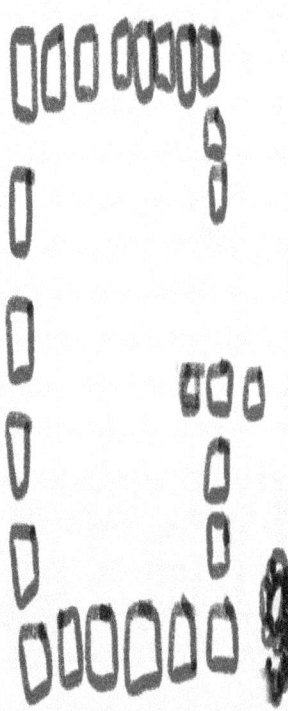

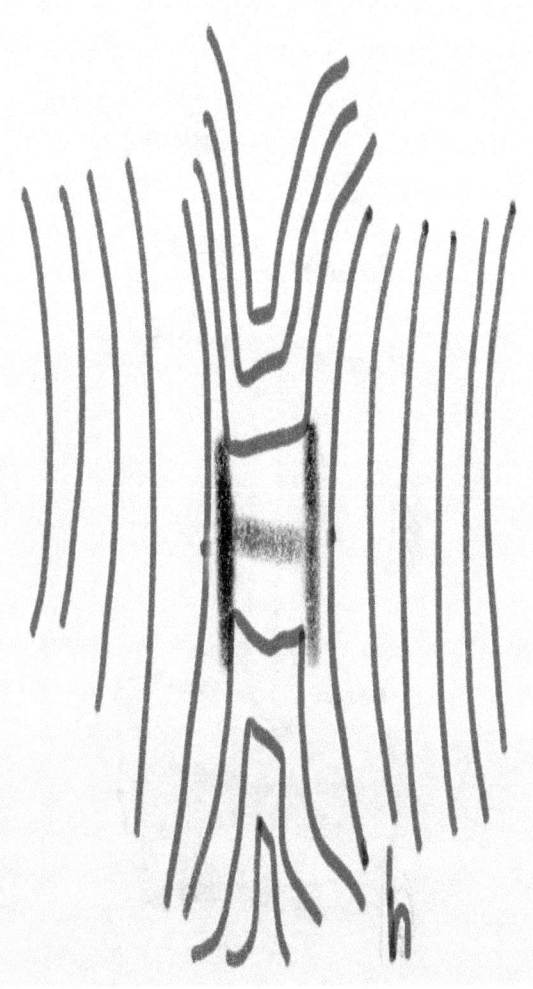

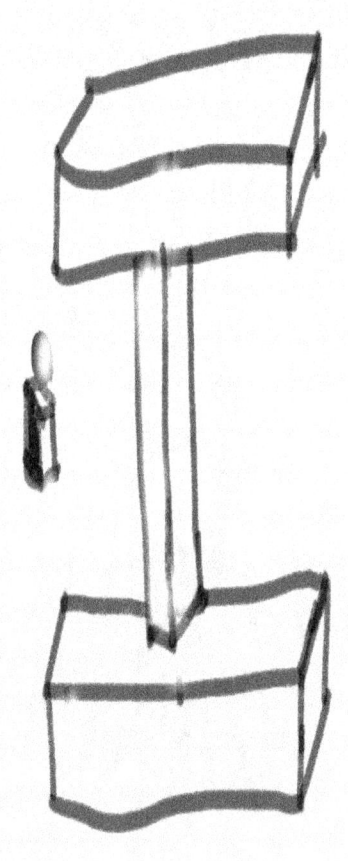

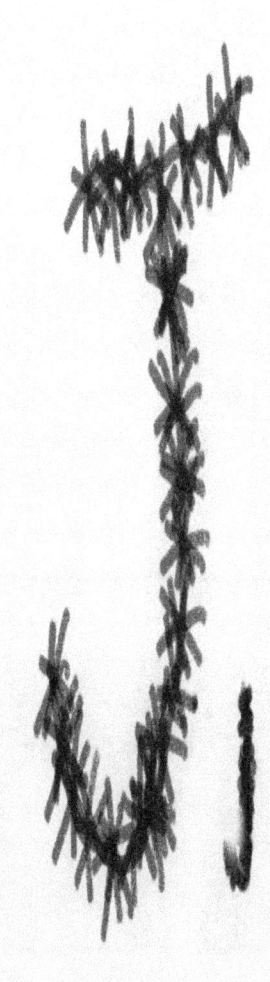

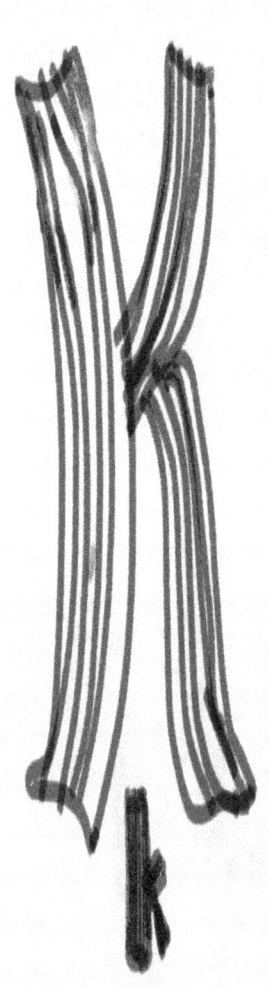

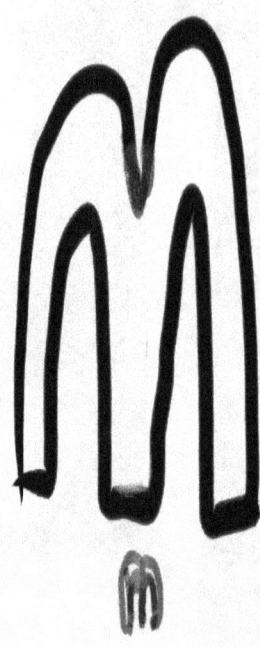

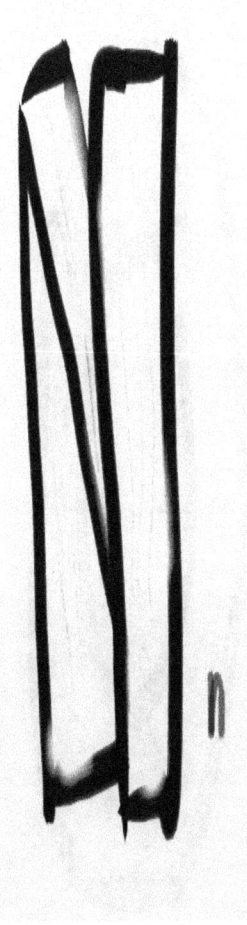

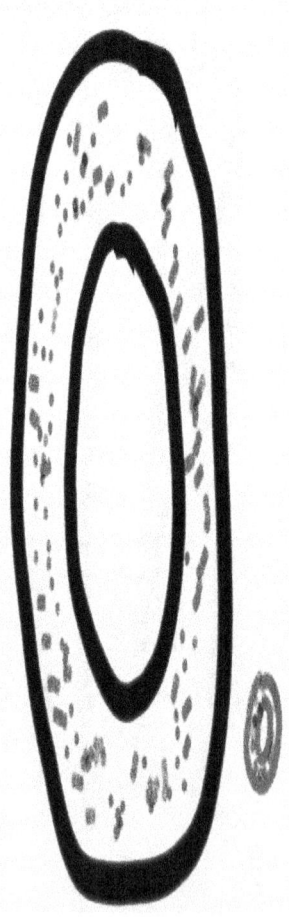

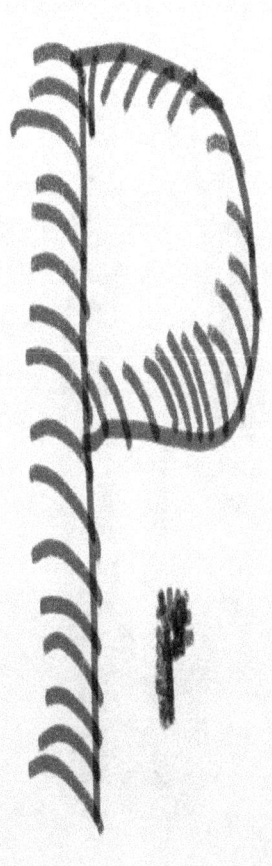

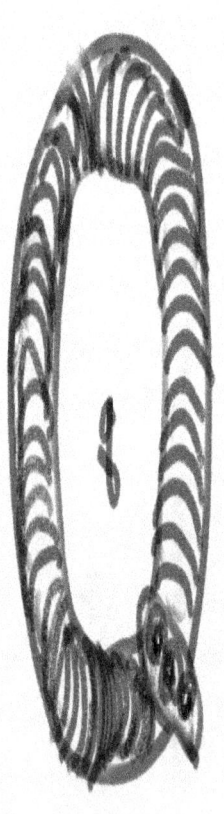

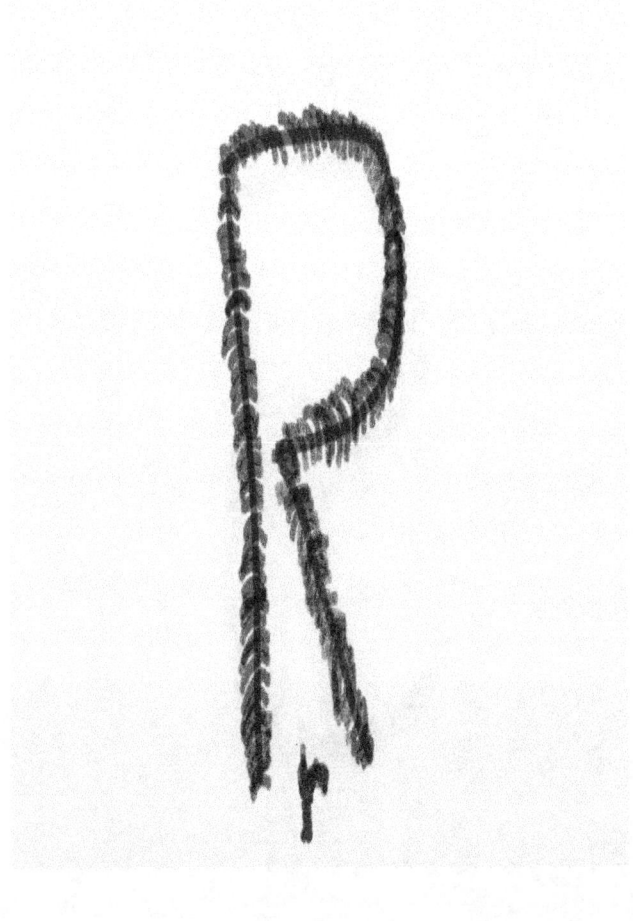

S

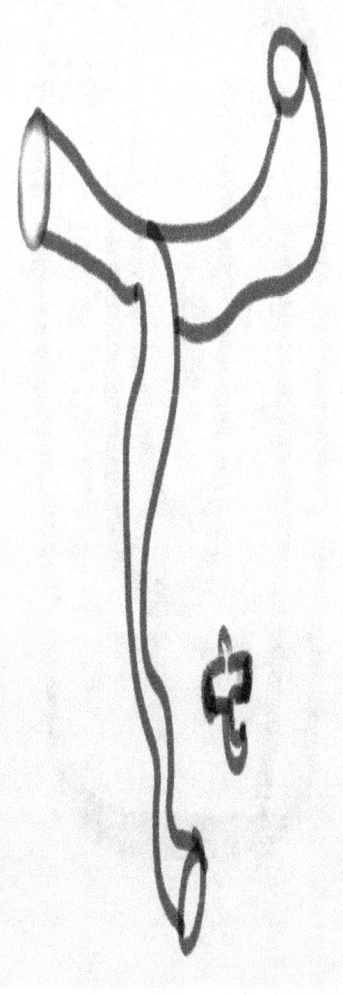

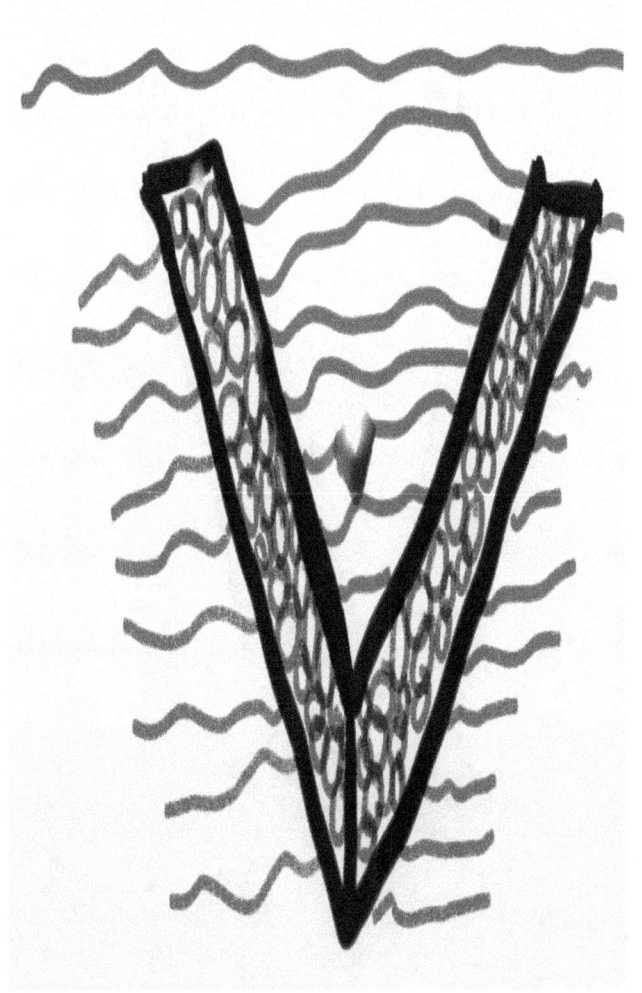

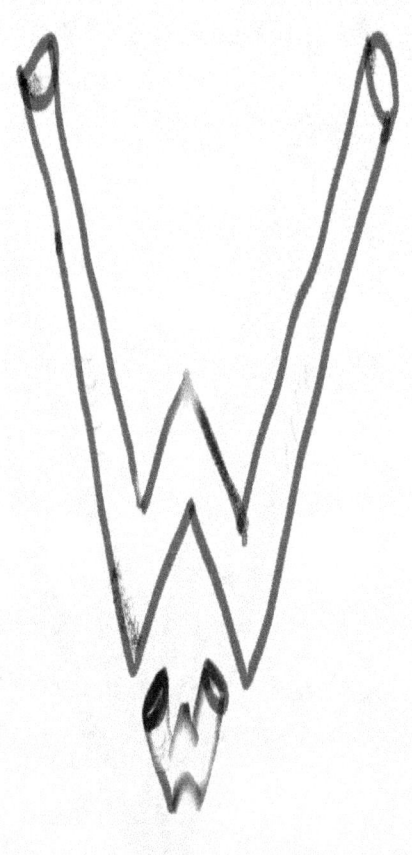

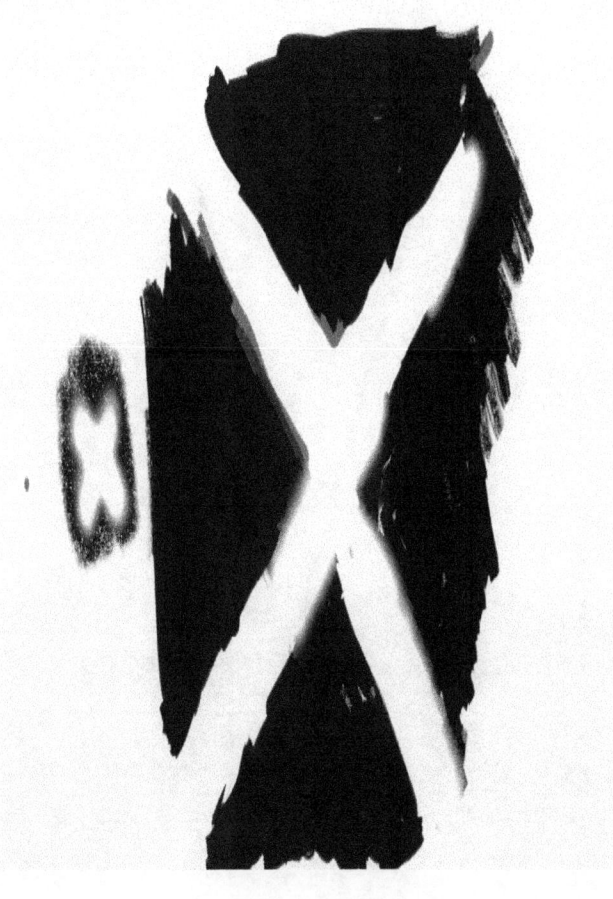

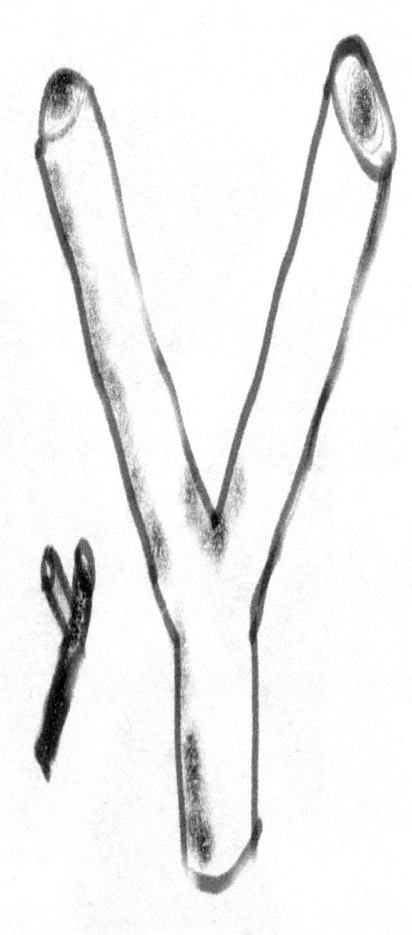

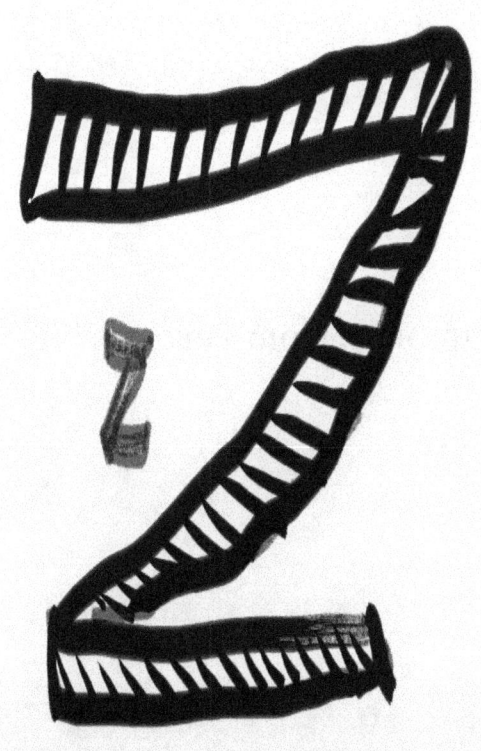

Numbers: from Zero to Nine

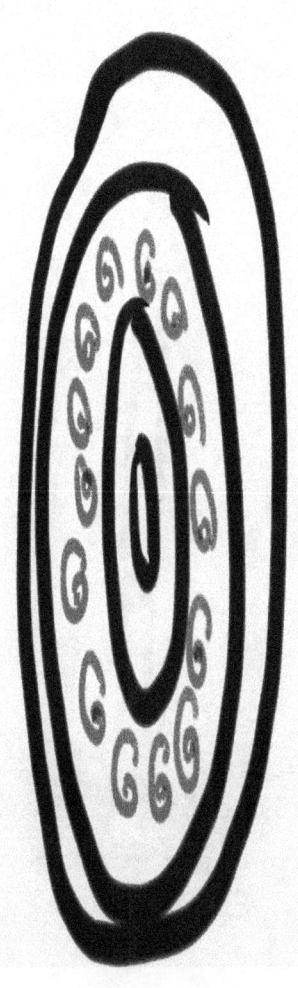

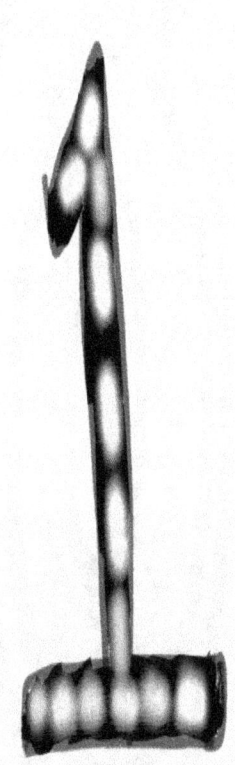

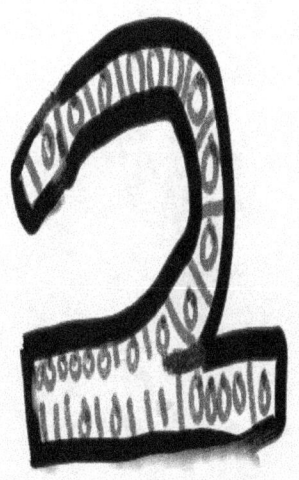

3

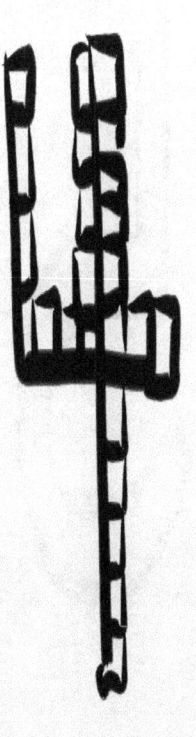

5

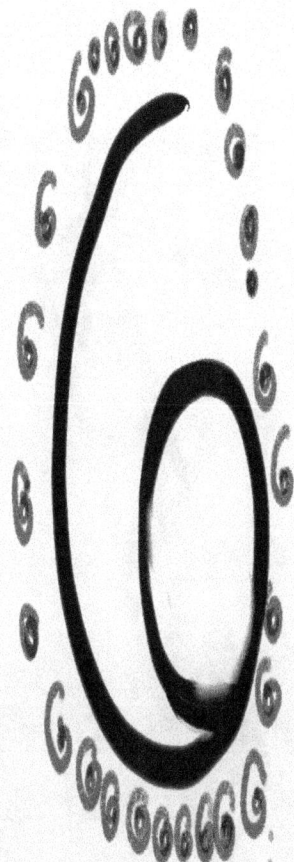

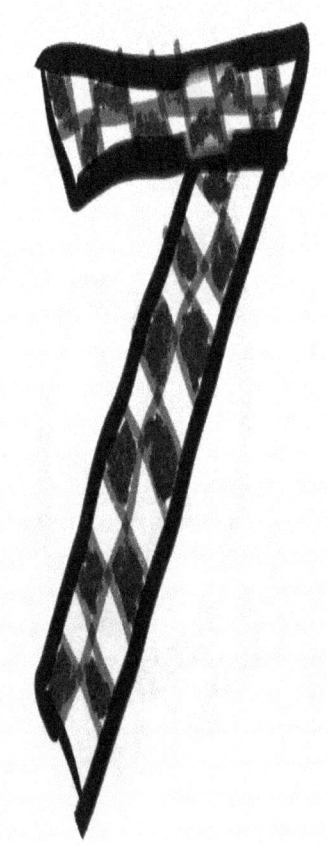

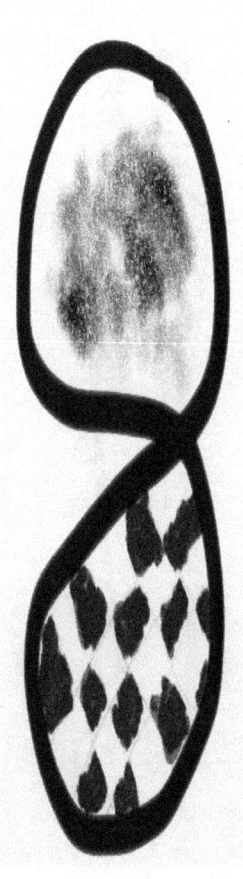

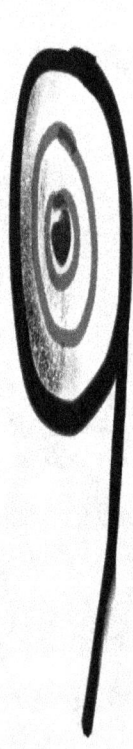

The End: So long and keep on doodling!